Austin Dobson, Hugh Thomson

The Ballad of Beau Brocade

And Other Poems of the 18th Century. Second Edition

Austin Dobson, Hugh Thomson

The Ballad of Beau Brocade

And Other Poems of the 18th Century. Second Edition

ISBN/EAN: 9783744713399

Printed in Europe, USA, Canada, Australia, Japan

Cover: Foto ©Thomas Meinert / pixelio.de

More available books at **www.hansebooks.com**

"She once had been the rage:—

The

Ballad of Beau Brocade

and
other Poems
of the XVIII th Century.

by

Austin Dobson

with
fifty Illustrations
by

Hugh Thomson

London
Kegan Paul,
Trench,
Trübner,
& Co.

MDCCCXCII

SECOND EDITION.

TO

LADY BOWEN.

'FOR OLD SAKE'S SAKE.'

' For old sake's sake!' 'Twere hard to choose
Words fitter for an old-world Muse
* Than these, that in their cadence bring*
* Faint fragrance of the posy-ring,*
And charms that rustic lovers use.

Life's journey lengthens, and we lose
The first pale flush, the morning hues,—
* Ah! but the back-look, lingering,*
*   For old sake's sake!*

That we retain. Though Time refuse
To lift the veil on forward views,
* Despot in most, he is not King*
* Of those kind memories that cling*
Around his travelled avenues
*   For old sake's sake!*

PREFATORY NOTE.

Concerning the eight pieces here reprinted from
" Old-World Idylls" *and* " At the Sign of the
Lyre," *it is only necessary to say that they have
been chosen because, being laid in the last Century, they appeared to present a congenial field
for the artistic ingenuity of Mr. Hugh Thomson,
who, notwithstanding the pressure of other duties,
has illustrated them with an ability which I can
only admire, and a personal enthusiasm for which
I can scarcely be sufficiently grateful.*

AUSTIN DOBSON.

September, 1892.

CONTENTS.

LIST OF ILLUSTRATIONS.

List of Illustrations. xiii

THE BALLAD OF BEAU BROCADE.

"Turned King's Evidence"

The Ballad of Beau Brocade

"Hark! I hear the Sound of Coaches"

I.

SEVENTEEN hundred and thirty-nine :—
That was the date of this tale of mine.

First great GEORGE was buried and gone;
GEORGE the Second was plodding on.

LONDON then, as the "Guides" aver,
Shared its glories with *Westminster :*

And people of rank, to correct their "tone,"
Went out of town to *Marybone.*

Those were the days of the War with *Spain,*
PORTO-BELLO would soon be ta'en :

WHITEFIELD preached to the colliers grim,
Bishops in lawn sleeves preached at him :

WALPOLE talked of "a man and his price" :
Nobody's virtue was over-nice :

Those, in fine, were the brave days when
Coaches were stopped by . . . *Highwaymen !*

And of all the knights of the gentle trade
Nobody bolder than "BEAU BROCADE."

This they knew on the whole way down :
Best,—maybe,—at the "*Oak and Crown.*"

Would 'Club' for a Guard

(For timorous cits on their pilgrimage

Would "club" for a "Guard" to ride the stage ;

And the Guard that rode on more than one

Was the Host of this hostel's sister's son.)

Open we here on a March-day fine,

Under the oak with the hanging sign.

.

There was Barber DICK with his basin by ;

Cobbler JOE with the patch on his eye ;

Portly product of Beef and Beer,

JOHN the host, he was standing near.

Straining and creaking, with wheels awry,

Lumbering came the "*Plymouth Fly*";—

Lumbering up from *Bagshot Heath*,

Guard in the basket armed to the teeth :

Passengers heavily armed inside :

Not the less surely the coach had been tried !

Tried!—but a couple of miles away,

By a well-dressed man!—in the open day!

Tried successfully, never a doubt,--

Pockets of passengers all turned out!

.

Cloak-bags rifled, and cushions ripped,--

Even an Ensign's wallet stripped!

Even a Methodist hosier's wife

Offered the choice of her Money or Life!

Highwayman's manners no less polite,

Hoped that their coppers (returned) were right;—

Sorry to find the company poor,

Hoped next time they'd travel with more;—

Plucked them all at his ease, in short:—

Such was the *"Plymouth Fly's"* report.

Sympathy ! horror ! and wonderment !

"Catch the Villain !"   (But Nobody went.)

where the best strong waters are

Hosier's wife led into the Bar :

(That 's where the best strong waters are !)

"Sympathy horror and wonderment"

Followed the tale of the hundred-and-one
Things that Somebody ought to have done.

Ensign (of BRAGG'S) made a terrible clangour:
But for the Ladies had drawn his hanger!

Robber, of course, was "BEAU BROCADE";
Out-spoke DOLLY the Chambermaid.

Devonshire DOLLY, plump and red,
Spoke from the gallery overhead:

Spoke it out boldly, staring hard:
"Why did n't you shoot then, GEORGE the Guard?"

Spoke it out bolder, seeing him mute:--
"GEORGE the Guard, why did n't you shoot?"

Portly JOHN grew pale and red,
(JOHN was afraid of her, people said :)

Gasped that " Dolly was surely cracked,"

(John was afraid of her—that 's a fact !)

George the Guard grew red and pale,

Slowly finished his quart of ale : —

" Shoot ?   Why—Rabbit him !—did n't he shoot ? "

Muttered— " The Baggage was far too 'cute !"

" Shoot ?   Why he 'd flashed the pan in his eye ! "

Muttered— " She 'd pay for it by and by ! "

Further than this made no reply.

Nor could a further reply be made.

For George was in league with " Beau Brocade " !

And John the Host, in his wakefullest state,

Was not—on the whole—immaculate.

But nobody's virtue was over-nice

When Walpole talked of "a man and his price" ;

●

Out-spoke Dolly the Chambermaid

George the Guard

And wherever Purity found abode,

'Twas certainly *not* on a posting road.

II

" Forty " followed to " Thirty-nine."

Glorious days of the *Hanover* line !

Princes were born, and drums were banged ;

Now and then batches of Highwaymen hanged.

" Glorious news ! "—from the *Spanish Main ;*

PORTO-BELLO at last was ta'en.

"Glorious news!"   for the liquor trade :

Nobody dreamed of " BEAU BROCADE."

People were thinking of *Spanish Crowns*,

Money was coming from seaport towns !

Nobody dreamed of " BEAU BROCADE,"

(Only DOLLY the Chambermaid !)

Blessings on VERNON !   Fill up the cans :

Money was coming in " *Flys* " and " *Vans.*"

Possibly, JOHN the Host had heard :

Also, certainly, GEORGE the Guard.

.

And DOLLY had possibly tidings, too,

That made her rise from her bed anew,

Plump as ever, but stern of eye,

With a fixed intention to warn the "*Fly.*"

"and drums were banged"

Lingering only at JOHN his door,

Just to make sure of a jerky snore :

"Saddling the Gray Mare"

Saddling the gray mare, *Dumpling Star;*

Fetching the pistol out of the bar :

(The old horse-pistol that, they say,

Came from the battle of *Malplaquet ;*)

Loading with powder that maids would use,

Even in " Forty," to clear the flues :

And a couple of silver buttons, the Squire

Gave her, away in *Devonshire.*

These she wadded for want of better

With the B   sh   p of L—nd—n's " Pastoral

    Letter " :

Looked to the flint, and hung the whole,

Ready to use, at her pocket-hole.

Thus equipped and accoutred, DOLLY

Clattered away to *"Exciseman's Folly" ;*

Such was the name of a ruined abode,

Just on the edge of the *London* road.

Thence she thought she might safely try,

As soon as she saw it, to warn the "*Fly.*"

Clattered away to Clarsemans Jelly

But, as chance fell out, her rein she drew,

As the BEAU came cantering into the view.

By the light of the moon she could see him drest

In his famous gold-sprigged tambour vest :

"Came Cantering up the road"

And under his silver-gray surtout,

The laced, historical coat of blue,

That he wore when he went to *London-Spaw*,

And robbed Sir MUNGO MUCKLETHRAW.

Out-spoke DOLLY the Chambermaid,

(Trembling a little, but not afraid,)

"Stand and Deliver, O 'BEAU BROCADE'!"

But the BEAU rode nearer, and would not speak,

For he saw by the moonlight a rosy cheek :

And a spavined mare with a rusty hide :

And a girl with her hand at her pocket-side.

So never a word he spoke as yet,

For he thought 'twas a freak of MEG or BET ;- -

A freak of the "*Rose*" or the "*Rummer*" set.

Out-spoke DOLLY the Chambermaid,

(Tremulous now, and sore afraid,)

"Stand and Deliver, O 'BEAU BROCADE'!" -

Firing then, out of sheer alarm,

Hit the BEAU in the bridle-arm.

Button the first went none knows where,

But it carried away his *solitaire :*

Button the second a circuit made,

Glanced in under the shoulder blade :

Down from the saddle fell " BEAU BROCADE." !

Down from the saddle and never stirred ! -

DOLLY grew white as a *Windsor* curd.

Slipped not less from the mare, and bound

Strips of her kirtle about his wound.

Then, lest his Worship should rise and flee,

Fettered his ankles   tenderly.

Jumped on his chestnut, BET the fleet

(Called after BET of *Portugal Street*) :

"Jotted her down on the spot."

Came like the wind to the old Inn-door ;—

Roused fat JOHN from a three-fold snore ;—

Vowed she 'd 'peach if he misbehaved . . .

Briefly, the "*Plymouth Fly*" was saved !

Staines and *Windsor* were all on fire :—

DOLLY was wed to a *Yorkshire* squire ;

Went to Town at the K—G's desire !

But whether His M—J—STY saw her or not,

HOGARTH jotted her down on the spot ;

And something of DOLLY one still may trace

In the fresh contours of his "*Milkmaid's*" face.

GEORGE the Guard fled over the sea :

JOHN had a fit—of perplexity ;

Turned King's evidence, sad to state :—

But JOHN was never immaculate.

As for the BEAU, he was duly tried,
When his wound was healed, at *Whitsuntide;*

Served—for a day—as the last of "sights,"
To the world of *St. James's-Street* and "*White's*",

Went on his way to TYBURN TREE,
With a pomp befitting his high degree.

Every privilege rank confers :—
Bouquet of pinks at *St. Sepulchre's;*

Flagon of ale at *Holborn Bar;*
Friends (in mourning) to follow his Car—
("t" is omitted where HEROES are!)

Every one knows the speech he made;
Swore that he "rather admired the Jade!"—

Waved to the crowd with his gold-laced hat :
Talked to the Chaplain after that;

Turned to the Topsman undismayed·. . .

This was the finish of " BEAU BROCADE " !

And this is the Ballad that seemed to hide

In the leaves of a dusty " LONDONER'S GUIDE ";

" Humbly Inscrib'd" (with curls and tails)

By the Author to FREDERICK, *Prince of* WALES :—

"Published by FRANCIS *and* OLIVER PINE ;

Ludgate-Hill, at the Blackmoor Sign.

Seventeen-Hundred-and-Thirty-Nine."

Ensign (of Bouquet)

A GENTLEMAN OF THE OLD SCHOOL.

"To catch
the Cuckoo's Call"

Hugh Thomson

Gentleman of the Old School

HE lived in that past Georgian day,
    When men were less inclined to say
That "Time is Gold," and overlay
    With toil their pleasure ;
He held some land, and dwelt thereon,—
Where, I forget,—the house is gone :
His Christian name, I think, was John,—
    His surname, Leisure.

Reynolds has painted him,—a face

Filled with a fine, old-fashioned grace,

Fresh-coloured, frank, with ne'er a trace

    Of trouble shaded ;

The eyes are blue, the hair is drest

In plainest way,—one hand is prest

Deep in a flapped canary vest,

    With buds brocaded.

He wears a brown old Brunswick coat,

With silver buttons,—round his throat,

A soft cravat :—in all you note

    An elder fashion,

A strangeness, which, to us who shine

In shapely hats,—whose coats combine

All harmonies of hue and line,

    Inspires compassion.

He lived so long ago, you see !

Men were untravelled then, but we,

Like Ariel, post o'er land and sea

  With careless parting ;

He found it quite enough for him

To smoke his pipe in "garden trim,"

And watch, about the fish tank's brim,

  The swallows darting.

He liked the well-wheel's creaking tongue,—
He liked the thrush that stopped and sung,—
He liked the drone of flies among
     His netted peaches :
He liked to watch the sunlight fall
Athwart his ivied orchard wall :
Or pause to catch the cuckoo's call
     Beyond the beeches.

His were the times of Paint and Patch,
And yet no Ranelagh could match
The sober doves that round his thatch
     Spread tails and sidled :
He liked their ruffling, puffed content,
For him their drowsy wheelings meant
More than a Mall of Beaux that bent,
     Or Belles that bridled.

Not that, in truth, when life began

He shunned the flutter of the fan :

He too had maybe "pinked his man "

    In Beauty's quarrel :

But now his "fervent youth " had flown

Where lost things go ; and he was grown

As staid and slow-paced as his own

    Old hunter, Sorrel.

Yet still he loved the chase, and held

That no composer's score excelled

'When Sweetlip swelled its Jovial Riot'

The merry horn, when Sweetlip swelled

Its jovial riot ;

But most his measured words of praise

Caressed the angler's easy ways,—

His idly meditative days, --

His rustic diet.

Not that his "meditating" rose
Beyond a sunny summer doze ;
He never troubled his repose
      With fruitless prying :
But held, as law for high and low,
What God withholds no man can know
And smiled away inquiry so,
      Without replying.

We read—alas, how much we read !—
The jumbled strifes of creed and creed
With endless controversies feed
      Our groaning tables :
His books—and they sufficed him— were
Cotton's "Montaigne," "The Grave" of Blair,
A "Walton"— much the worse for wear,
      And ".Esop's Fables."

One more,—"The Bible."   Not that he

Had searched its page as deep as we ;

No sophistries could make him see

      Its slender credit ;

It may be that he could not count

The sires and sons to Jesse's fount, —

He liked the "Sermon on the Mount,"—

      And more, he read it.

Once he had loved, but failed to wed,

A red-cheeked lass who long was dead ;

His ways were far too slow, he said,

      To quite forget her ;

And still when time had turned him gray,

The earliest hawthorn buds in May

Would find his lingering feet astray,

      Where first he met her.

"*In Cœlo Quies*" heads the stone

On Leisure's grave,—now little known,

A tangle of wild-rose has grown

    So thick across it ;

Scrret

The "Benefactions" still declare

He left the clerk an elbow-chair,

And "12 Pence Yearly to Prepare

    A Christmas Posset."

Lie softly, Leisure!   Doubtless you,

With too serene a conscience drew

Your easy breath, and slumbered through

       The gravest issue ;

But we, to whom our age allows

Scarce space to wipe our weary brows,

Look down upon your narrow house,

       Old friend, and miss you !

A GENTLEWOMAN OF THE OLD SCHOOL.

'She'd still her beau,

SHE lived in Georgian era too.

Most women then, if bards be
true,

Succumbed to Routs and Cards, or grew

Devout and acid.

But hers was neither fate.   She came

Of good west-country folk, whose fame

Has faded now.   For us her name

Is " Madam Placid."

Patience or Prudence,—what you will,

Some prefix faintly fragrant still

As those old musky scents that fill

      Our grandams' pillows ;

And for her youthful portrait take

Some long-waist child of Hudson's make,

Stiffly at ease beside a lake

      With swans and willows.

I keep her later semblance placed

Beside my desk,—'tis lawned and laced,

In shadowy sanguine stipple traced

      By Bartolozzi :

A placid face, in which surprise

Is seldom seen, but yet there lies

Some vestige of the laughing eyes

      Of arch Piozzi.

For her e'en Time grew debonair.

He, finding cheeks unclaimed of care,

With late-delayed faint roses there,

      And lingering dimples,

Had spared to touch the fair old face,

And only kissed with Vauxhall grace

The soft white hand that stroked her lace,

      Or smoothed her wimples.

So left her beautiful.   Her age

Was comely as her youth was sage,

And yet she once had been the rage ;—

      It hath been hinted,

Indeed, affirmed by one or two,

Some spark at Bath (as sparks will do)

Inscribed a song to " Lovely Prue,"

      Which Urban printed.

I know she thought; I know she felt;

Perchance could sum, I doubt she spelt;

She knew as little of the Celt

    -    As of the Saxon;

I know she played and sang, for yet

We keep the tumble-down spinet

To which she quavered ballads set

    By Arne or Jackson.

Her tastes were not refined as ours;

She liked plain food and homely flowers,

Refused to paint, kept early hours,

    Went clad demurely;

Her art was sampler-work design,

Fireworks for her were "vastly fine,"

Her luxury was elder-wine,—

    She loved that "purely."

Hè. Thomson
Aug 92.

"The
warm west-looking window-seat."

She was renowned, traditions say,

For June conserves, for curds and whey,

For finest tea (she called it "tay"),

And ratafia ;

She knew, for sprains, what bands to choose,

Could tell the sovereign wash to use

For freckles, and was learned in brews

As erst Medea.

Yet studied little.   She would read,

On Sundays, " Pearson on the Creed,"

Though, as I think, she could not heed

His text profoundly ;

Seeing she chose for her retreat

The warm west-looking window-seat,

Where, if you chanced to raise your feet,

You slumbered soundly.

This, 'twixt ourselves.　The dear old dame,

In truth, was not so much to blame ;

The excellent divine I name

　　　　Is scarcely stirring :

Her plain-song piety preferred

Pure life to precept.　If she erred,

She knew her faults.　Her softest word

　　　　Was for the erring.

If she had loved, or if she kept

Some ancient memory green, or wept

Over the shoulder-knot that slept

　　　　Within her cuff-box,

I know not.　Only this I know,

At sixty-five she'd still her beau,

A lean French exile, lame and slow,

　　　　With monstrous snuff-box.

Hugh
Thomson

"Delighted in his dry bon-mots
And cackling laughter,"

Younger than she, well-born and bred.

She 'd found him in St. Giles', half dead

Of teaching French for nightly bed

       And daily dinners ;

Starving, in fact, 'twixt want and pride ;

And so, henceforth, you always spied

His rusty " pigeon-wings " beside

       Her Mechlin pinners.

.

He worshipped her, you may suppose.

She gained him pupils, gave him clothes,

Delighted in his dry bon-mots

       And cackling laughter ;

And when, at last, the long duet

Of conversation and picquet

Ceased with her death, of sheer regret

       He died soon after.

Dear Madam Placid!   Others knew

Your worth as well as he, and threw

Their flowers upon your coffin too,

      I take for granted.

Their loves are lost ; but still we see

Your kind and gracious memory

Bloom yearly with the almond tree

      The Frenchman planted.

The Almond Tree

A DEAD LETTER.

"By the broken Stile."

A Dead Letter.

A cœur blessé—l'ombre et le silence
H. de Balzac.

I

I DREW it from its china tomb;—
    It came out feebly scented
With some thin ghost of past
        perfume
That dust and days had lent it.

An old, old letter,—folded still!
    To read with due composure,
I sought the sun-lit window-sill,
    Above the gray enclosure,

That glimmering in the sultry haze,

    Faint-flowered, dimly shaded,

Slumbered like Goldsmith's Madam Blaize,

    Bedizened and brocaded.

A queer old place! You 'd surely say

    Some tea-board garden-maker

Had planned it in Dutch William's day

    To please some florist Quaker,

So trim it was. The yew-trees still,

    With pious care perverted,

Grew in the same grim shapes ; and still

    The lipless dolphin spurted ;

Still in his wonted state abode

    The broken-nosed Apollo :

And still the cypress-arbour showed

    The same umbrageous hollow.

Only,—as fresh young Beauty gleams
  From coffee-coloured laces,—
So peeped from its old-fashioned dreams
  The fresher modern traces :

For idle mallet, hoop, and ball
  Upon the lawn were lying ;
A magazine, a tumbled shawl,
  Round which the swifts were flying ;

And tossed beside the Guelder rose,
  A heap of rainbow knitting,
Where, blinking in her pleased repose,
  A Persian cat was sitting.

"A place to love in,—live,—for aye,
  If we too, like Tithonus,
Could find some God to stretch the gray,
  Scant life the Fates have thrown us ;

" But now by steam we run our race,

  With buttoned heart and pocket ;

Our Love 's a gilded, surplus grace,—

  Just like an empty locket !

" ' The time is out of joint.' Who will,

  May strive to make it better ;

For me, this warm old window-sill,

  And this old dusty letter."

II.

" Dear *John* (the letter ran), it can't, can't be,

  For Father 's gone to *Chorley Fair* with *Sam*,

And Mother 's storing Apples, *Prue* and Me

  Up to our Elbows making Damson Jam :

But we shall meet before a Week is gone,—

  '"Tis a long Lane that has no Turning,' *John !*

"Sam's two Eyes are all for
Cissy

Hugh Thomson

" Only till Sunday next, and then you 'll wait

    Behind the White-Thorn, by the broken Stile—

We can go round and catch them at the Gate,

    All to Ourselves, for nearly one long Mile ;

Dear *Prue* won't look, and Father he 'll go on,

And *Sam's* two Eyes are all for *Cissy, John !*

" *John*, she 's so smart,—with every Ribbon new,

    Flame-coloured Sack, and Crimson Padesoy :

As proud as proud ; and has the Vapours too,

    Just like My Lady ;—calls poor *Sam* a Boy,

And vows no Sweet-heart 's worth the Thinking-on

Till he 's past Thirty . . . I know better, *John !*

" My Dear, I don't think that I thought of much

    Before we knew each other, I and you ;

And now, why, *John*, your least, least Finger-touch,

    Gives me enough to think a Summer through.

See, for I send you Something !   There, 'tis gone !

Look in this corner,—mind you find it, *John !*"

III.

This was the matter of the note,

    A long-forgot deposit,

Dropped in an Indian dragon's throat,

    Deep in a fragrant closet.

Piled with a dapper Dresden world,—

    Beaux, beauties, prayers, and poses, —

Bonzes with squat legs undercurled,

    And great jars filled with roses.

Ah, heart that wrote !   Ah, lips that kissed

    You had no thought or presage

Into what keeping you dismissed

    Your simple old-world message !

A reverent one.   Though we to-day
   Distrust beliefs and powers,
The artless, ageless things you say
   Are fresh as May's own flowers,

Starring some pure primeval spring,
   Ere Gold had grown despotic,—
Ere Life was yet a selfish thing,
   Or Love a mere exotic !

I need not search too much to find
   Whose lot it was to send it,
That feel upon me yet the kind,
   Soft hand of her who penned it ;

And see, through two score years of smoke,
   In by-gone, quaint apparel,
Shine from yon time-black Norway oak
   The face of Patience Caryl,—

The pale, smooth forehead, silver-tressed :
  The gray gown, primly flowered :
The spotless, stately coif whose crest
  Like Hector's horse-plume towered :

And still the sweet half-solemn look
  Where some past thought was clinging,
As when one shuts a serious book
  To hear the thrushes singing.

I kneel to you ! Of those you were,
  Whose kind old hearts grow mellow,—
Whose fair old faces grow more fair
  As Point and Flanders yellow :

Whom some old store of garnered grief,
  Their placid temples shading,
Crowns like a wreath of autumn leaf
  With tender tints of fading.

Peace to your soul! You died unwed—

    Despite this loving letter.

And what of John? The less that's said

    Of John, I think, the better.

THE OLD SEDAN CHAIR.

"As he lifts he out light"

" What's not destroy'd by Time's devouring Hand?
Where's Troy, and where's the May-Pole in the Strand?"
BRAMSTON'S "ART OF POLITICKS."

I'T stands in the stable-yard, under the eaves,

. Propped up by a broom-stick and covered with

leaves :

It once was the pride of the gay and the fair.

But now 'tis a ruin,—that old Sedan chair !

It is battered and tattered,—it little avails

That once it was lacquered, and glistened with nails;

For its leather is cracked into lozenge and square,

Like a canvas by Wilkie,—that old Sedan chair!

See,—here came the bearing-straps; here were the
　　　holes

For the poles of the bearers—when once there were
　　　poles:

It was cushioned with silk, it was wadded with hair,

As the birds have discovered,—that old Sedan chair!

"Where's Troy?" says the poet! Look, under the
　　　seat,

Is a nest with four eggs,—'tis the favoured retreat

Of the Muscovy hen, who has hatched, I dare swear,

Quite an army of chicks in that old Sedan chair!

"But prone, on a question
of fare

And yet—Can't you fancy a face in the frame
Of the window,—some high-headed damsel or dame,
Be-patched and be-powdered, just set by the stair,
While they raise up the lid of that old Sedan chair?

Can't you fancy Sir Plume, as beside her he stands,
With his ruffles a-droop on his delicate hands,
With his cinnamon coat, with his laced solitaire,
As he lifts her out light from that old Sedan chair?

Then it swings away slowly.   Ah, many a league
It has trotted 'twixt sturdy-legged Terence and Teague:
Stout fellows!—but prone, on a question of fare,
To brandish the poles of that old Sedan chair!

It has waited by portals where Garrick has played;
It has waited by Heidegger's "Grand Masquerade:"
For my Lady Codille, for my Lady Bellair,
It has waited—and waited, that old Sedan chair!

Oh, the scandals it knows! Oh, the tales it could tell

Of Drum and Ridotto, of Rake and of Belle,

Of Cock-fight and Levee, and (scarcely more rare!)

Of Fête-days at Tyburn, that old Sedan chair!

"*Heu! quantum mutata,*" I say as I go.

It deserves better fate than a stable-yard, though!

We must furbish it up, and dispatch it,—"With Care,"—

To a Fine-Art Museum—that old Sedan chair!

THE LADIES OF ST. JAMES'S.

"They frown on you—for weeks"

The Ladies of St. James's
A Proper New Ballad of the Country and the Town

"_Phyllida amo ante alias._"
VIRG.

THE ladies of St. James's

   Go swinging to the play:

Their footmen run before them,

   With a "Stand by! Clear the way!"

But Phyllida, my Phyllida!

   She takes her buckled shoon,

When we go out a-courting

   Beneath the harvest moon.

F

The ladies of St. James's
    Wear satin on their backs ;
They sit all night at *Ombre*,
    With candles all of wax :
But Phyllida, my Phyllida !
    She dons her russet gown,
And runs to gather May dew
    Before the world is down.

The ladies of St. James's !
    They are so fine and fair,
You 'd think a box of essences
    Was broken in the air :
But Phyllida, my Phyllida !
    The breath of heath and furze,
When breezes blow at morning,
    Is not so fresh as hers.

H Thomson
1 Aug 92

Sylvia runs to gather May Dew

The ladies of St. James's !

   They're painted to the eyes ;

The white it stays for ever,

   Their red it never dies :

But Phyllida, my Phyllida !

   Her colour comes and goes ;

It trembles to a lily,—

   It wavers to a rose.

The ladies of St. James's !

   You scarce can understand

The half of all their speeches,

   Their phrases are so grand :

But Phyllida, my Phyllida !

   Her shy and simple words

Are clear as after rain-drops

   The music of the birds.

The ladies of St. James's!
　They have their fits and freaks :
They smile on you - for seconds,
　They frown on you -for weeks :
But Phyllida, my Phyllida !
　Come either storm or shine,
From Shrove-tide unto Shrove-tide,
　Is always true   and mine.

My Phyllida ! my Phyllida !
　I care not though they heap
The hearts of all St. James's,
　And give me all to keep :
I care not whose the beauties
　Of all the world may be,
For Phyllida -- for Phyllida
　Is all the world to me !

MOLLY TREFUSIS.

"Has she wooed?"

Molly Trefusis.

"Now the Graces are four and the Venuses two,
And ten is the number of Muses;
For a Muse and a Grace and a Venus are you
My dear little Molly Trefusis!"

So he wrote, the old bard of an "old magazine:"

As a study it not without use is,
If we wonder a moment who she may have been,
This same "little Molly Trefusis!"

She was Cornish.   We know that at once by the "Tre;"
Then of guessing it scarce an abuse is
If we say that where Bude bellows back to the sea
Was the birthplace of Molly Trefusis.

And she lived in the era of patches and bows,

 Not knowing what rouge or ceruse is;

For they needed (I trust) but her natural rose,

 The lilies of Molly Trefusis.

And I somehow connect her (I frankly admit

 That the evidence hard to produce is)

With BATH in its hey-day of Fashion and Wit,—

 This dangerous Molly Trefusis.

I fancy her, radiant in ribbon and knot,

 (How charming that old-fashioned puce is!)

All blooming in laces, fal-lals and what not,

 At the PUMP ROOM,—Miss Molly Trefusis.

I fancy her reigning,—a Beauty,— a Toast,

 Where BLADUD's medicinal cruse is;

And we know that at least of one Bard it could boast,—

 The Court of Queen Molly Trefusis.

Miss Molly Trefusis

He says she was " VENUS."   I doubt it.   Beside,

   (Your rhymer so hopelessly loose is !)

His " little " could scarce be to Venus applied,

   If fitly to Molly Trefusis.

No, no.   It was HEBE he had in his mind :

   And fresh as the handmaid of Zeus is,

And rosy, and rounded, and dimpled, —you'll find,—

   Was certainly Molly Trefusis !

Then he calls her "a MUSE."   To the charge I reply

   That we all of us know what a Muse is :

It is something too awful,—-too acid,—too dry,—

   For sunny-eyed Molly Trefusis.

But "a GRACE."   There I grant he was probably right ;

   (The rest but a verse-making ruse is)

It was all that was graceful,—intangible,—-light,

   The beauty of Molly Trefusis !

Was she wooed? Who can hesitate much about that
    Assuredly more than obtuse is ;
For how could the poet have written so pat
    " *My* dear little Molly Trefusis ! "

And was wed? That I think we must plainly infer,
    Since of suitors the common excuse is
To take to them Wives.   So it happened to her,
    Of course,—"little Molly Trefusis ! "

To the Bard? 'Tis unlikely.   Apollo, you see,
    In practical matters a goose is :—
'Twas a knight of the shire, and a hunting J.P.,
    Who carried off Molly Trefusis !

And you 'll find, I conclude, in the "*Gentleman's Mag.*,"
    At the end, where the pick of the news is,
" *On the* (blank), *at ' the Bath,' to Sir Hilary Bragg,*
    With a Fortune, Miss Molly Trefusis."

"'Twas a knight of the shire"

Thereupon . . But no farther the student may pry:

Love's temple is dark as Eleusis;

So here, at the threshold, we part, you and I,

From "dear little Molly Trefusis."

A CHAPTER OF FROISSART.

An ivy-leaf for "Orchard corner"

A Chapter of Froissart

YOU don't know Froissart now, young folks,

This age, I think, prefers recitals

Of high-spiced crime, with "slang" for jokes,

And startling titles :

But, in my time, when still some few

Loved "old Montaigne," and praised Pope's *Homer*

(Nay, thought to style him "poet" too,

Were scarce misnomer),

Sir John was less ignored.   Indeed,
 I can re-call how Some-one present
(Who spoils her grandson, Frank!) would read,
  And find him pleasant :

For,—by this copy,   hangs a Tale.
 Long since, in an old house in Surrey,
Where men knew more of " morning ale "
  Than " Lindley Murray,"

In a dim-lighted, whip-hung hall.
 'Neath Hogarth's " Midnight Conversation,"
It stood : and oft 'twixt spring and fall.
  With fond elation.

I turned the brown old leaves.   For there
 All through one hopeful happy summer,
At such a page (I well knew where).
  Some secret comer,

Whom I can picture, 'Trix, like you

   (Though scarcely such a colt unbroken),

Would sometimes place for private view

      A certain token ;—

A rose-leaf meaning "Garden Wall,"

   An ivy-leaf for "Orchard corner,"

A thorn to say, "Don't come at all,"—

      Unwelcome warner !—

Not that, in truth, our friends gainsaid ;

   But then Romance required dissembling,

(Ann Radcliffe taught us that !) which bred

      Some genuine trembling ;

Though, as a rule, all used to end

   In such kind confidential parley

As may to you kind Fortune send,

      You long-legged Charlie,

When your time comes.   How years slip on !

We had our crosses like our betters ;

Fate sometimes looked askance upon

Those floral letters ;

And once, for three long days disdained,

The dust upon the folio settled ;

For some-one, in the right, was pained,

And some-one nettled,

That sure was in the wrong, but spake

Of fixed intent and purpose stony

To serve King George, enlist and make

Minced-meat of " Boney,"

Who yet survived –ten years at least.

And so, when she I mean came hither

One day that need for letters ceased,

She brought this with her.

Here is the leaf-stained Chapter :—*How*

   The English King laid Siege to Calais ;

I think Gran. knows it even now,—

     Go ask her, Alice.

NOTES.

NOTES.

NOTE 1, PAGE 7.

"Ensign (of BRAGG'S) *made a terrible clangour."*

DESPITE its suspicious appropriateness in this case, " Bragg's " regiment of Foot-Guards really existed, and was ordered to Flanders in April, 1742 (see *Gentleman's Magazine*, 1742, i. 217).

NOTE 2, PAGE 9.

" PORTO-BELLO *at last was ta'en."*

Porto-Bello was taken in November, 1739. But Vice-Admiral Vernon's despatches did not reach England until the following March (see *Gentleman's Magazine* for 1740, i. 124, *et seq.*).

NOTE 3, PAGE 17.

" In the fresh contours of his ' Milkmaid's *' face."*

See Hogarth's *Enraged Musician*, an engraving of which was published in November of the following year (1741). To annotate this Ballad more fully would be easy ; but the reader will perhaps take the details for granted. In answer to some enquiries, it may, however, be stated that there is no foundation in fact for the story.

NOTE 4, PAGE 61.

" To brandish the poles of that old Sedan Chair!"

A friendly critic, whose versatile pen it is not easy to mistake, recalls, *à-propos* of the above, the following passage from Molière, which shows that Chairmen are much the same all the world over :—

" 1 Porteur (prenant un des bâtons de sa chaise). *Çà, payez nous vîtement!*

Mascarille. *Quoi?*

1 Porteur. *Je dis que je veux avoir de l'argent tout à l'heure.*

Mascarille. *Il est raisonnable, celui-là,"* etc.

Les Précieuses Ridicules, Sc. vii.

NOTE 5, PAGE 71.

MOLLY TREFUSIS.

The epigram here quoted from "an old magazine" is to be found in the late Lord Neaves's admirable little volume, *The Greek Anthology* (Blackwood's *Ancient Classics for English Readers*). Those familiar with eighteenth-century literature will recognize in the verses that follow but another echo of those lively stanzas of John Gay to "Molly Mogg of the Rose," which found so many imitators in his own day.

Whether my heroine is to be identified with a certain "Miss Trefusis" whose poems are sometimes to be found in the second-hand booksellers' catalogues, I know not. But if she is, I trust I have done her accomplished shade no wrong.